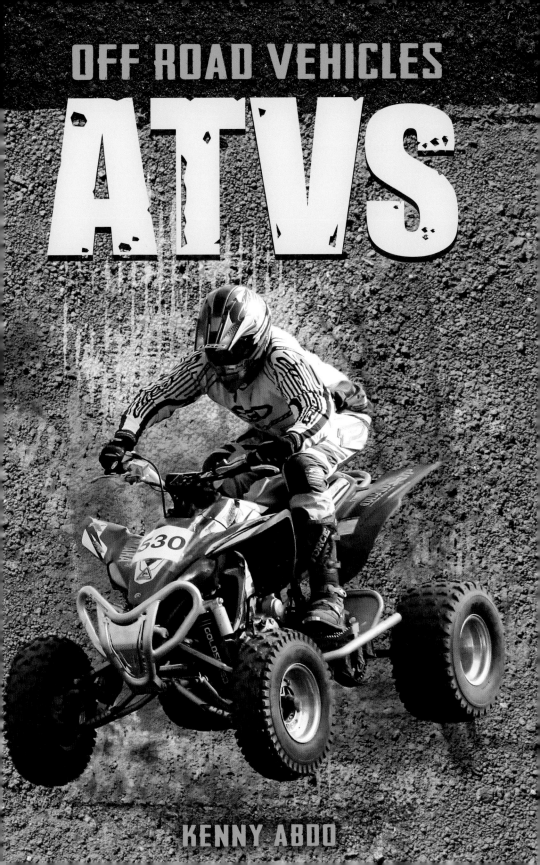

OFF ROAD VEHICLES
ATVS

KENNY ABDO

abdopublishing.com

Published by Abdo Zoom, a division of ABDO, P.O. Box 398166, Minneapolis, Minnesota 55439. Copyright © 2018 by Abdo Consulting Group, Inc. International copyrights reserved in all countries. No part of this book may be reproduced in any form without written permission from the publisher.

Printed in the United States of America, North Mankato, Minnesota.
092017
012018

Photo Credits: iStock, Shutterstock
Production Contributors: Kenny Abdo, Jennie Forsberg, Grace Hansen
Design Contributors: Dorothy Toth, Neil Klinepier

Publisher's Cataloging-in-Publication Data

Names: Abdo, Kenny, author.
Title: ATVs / by Kenny Abdo.
Description: Minneapolis, Minnesota: Abdo Zoom, 2018. | Series: Off road vehicles
     Includes online resource and index.
Identifiers: LCCN 2017939269 | ISBN 9781532120992 (lib.bdg.)
     ISBN 9781532122118 (ebook) | ISBN 9781532122675 (Read-to-Me ebook)
Subjects: LCSH: all terrain vehicles--Juvenile literature.
     Vehicles--Juvenile literature. | Motor Sports—Juvenile literature.
Classification: DDC 629.22042--dc23
LC record available at https://lccn.loc.gov/2017939269

TABLE OF CONTENTS

ATV

All terrain vehicles (ATVs) are built to drive on different types of land, like sand and mud.

ATVs are driven off-road.
They are hard to drive on
paved roads.

TYPES

ATVs are for one person to drive. Some can seat two people. These are called **tandem** ATVs.

ATVs have either three or four wheels, which help move through many types of land.

ATVs use off-road tires known as knobby tires. Knobbies use deep tread to drive better on unpaved terrains like gravel and mud.

ATVs are used in many ways for their off-roading ability. These include construction, law enforcement, and military.

ATVs are made for all types of racing like Motocross, desert racing, and hill climbing.

Sport models are built to be lightweight, high-powered, and lower to the ground. They are used for racing.

ATV races usually include
big jumps, tight corners,
and tricks.

GLOSSARY

military – a country's armed forces.

Motocross – form of off-road racing with motorcycles on enclosed tracks.

off-road – riding a vehicle on difficult roads or tracks, like sand, mud, or gravel.

tandem – a vehicle with matching parts, like seats, arranged one behind the other.

terrain – a piece of land having certain features.

tread – the part of a wheel that touches the ground.

ONLINE RESOURCES

Booklinks
NONFICTION NETWORK
FREE! ONLINE NONFICTION RESOURCES

To learn more about ATVs, please visit abdobooklinks.com. These links are routinely monitored and updated to provide the most current information available.

INDEX